This book
belongs to:

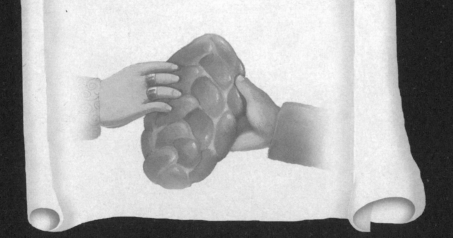

In God's Hands

Lawrence Kushner and Gary Schmidt
Illustrations by Matthew J. Baek

For Zella and Bluma, God's laughter

—L.K.

For Cheryl Hoogstrate, one of God's hands

— G.S.

Now to our God and Father be glory
forever and ever. Amen.

—M.J.B.

In God's Hands
2005 First Printing
Text © 2005 by Lawrence Kushner and Gary Schmidt
Illustrations © 2005 by Matthew J. Baek

For information regarding permission to reprint material from this book, please mail or
fax your request in writing to Jewish Lights Publishing, Permissions Department, at the
address / fax number listed below, or e-mail your request to permissions@
jewishlights.com.

Library of Congress Cataloging-in-Publication Data
Kushner, Lawrence, 1943–
In God's hands / Lawrence Kushner, Gary Schmidt ; illustrated by Matthew J. Baek.
p. cm.
Summary: While contemplating their problems in a synagogue, Jacob and David, one
man rich, the other poor, come to realize their role in making miracles happen.
Inspired by an ancient legend.
ISBN 1-58023-224-8 (hardcover)
[1. Miracles—Fiction. 2. Jews—Fiction. 3. Synagogues—Fiction. 4. Prayer—Fiction.] I.
Schmidt, Gary D. II. Baek, Matthew J., 1971–, ill. III. Title.
PZ7.K96438 2005
[E]—dc22

2005001669

Manufactured in China
Interior & jacket design: Jenny Buono

For People of All Faiths, All Backgrounds
Published by Jewish Lights Publishing
A Division of LongHill Partners, Inc.
Sunset Farm Offices, Route 4, P.O. Box 237
Woodstock, VT 05091
Tel: (802) 457-4000   Fax: (802) 457-4004
www.jewishlights.com

When the sun sets and stars fill the sky, the square in the little town grows quiet and still. The cool air of distant hills mingles with the sweet scent of baking bread. The moon rises and glows softly. It's the sort of place where miracles could happen.

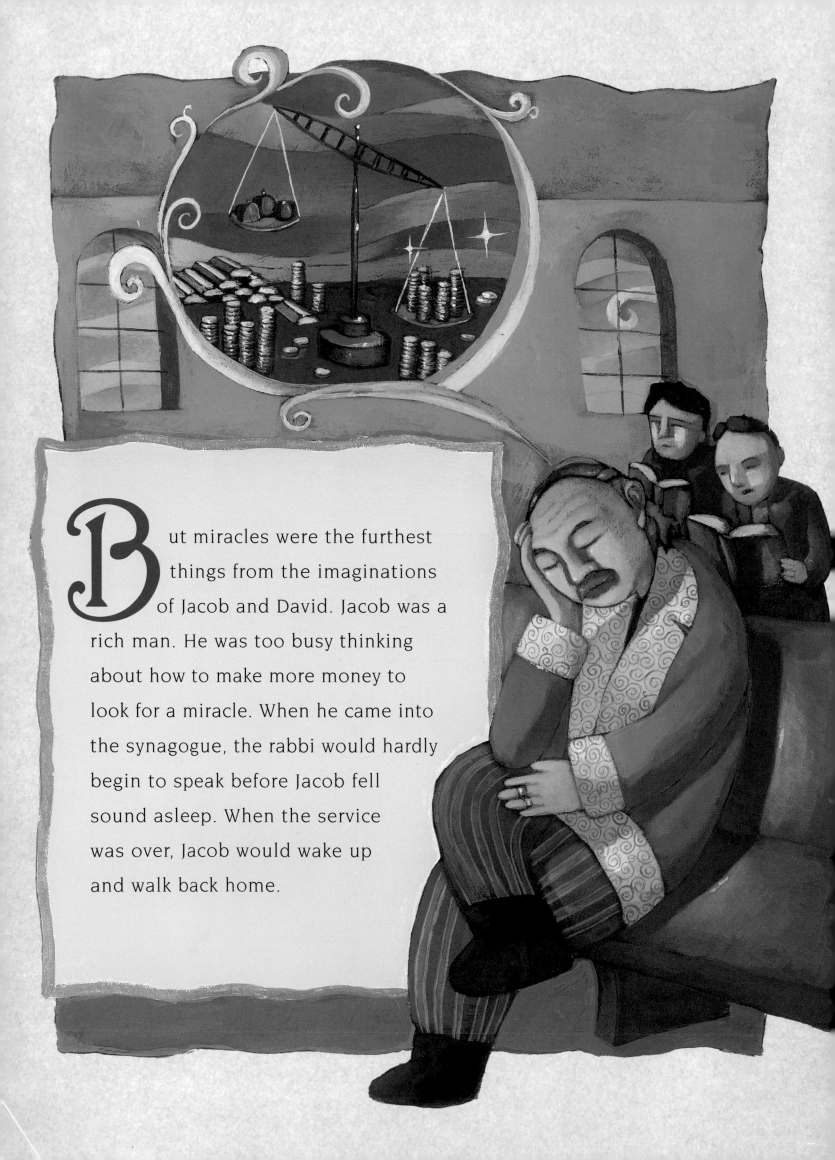

But miracles were the furthest things from the imaginations of Jacob and David. Jacob was a rich man. He was too busy thinking about how to make more money to look for a miracle. When he came into the synagogue, the rabbi would hardly begin to speak before Jacob fell sound asleep. When the service was over, Jacob would wake up and walk back home.

David was a poor man. He was too busy thinking about how to feed his family to look for a miracle. He was the caretaker at the synagogue. When the prayers were done, he would sweep and dust and tidy up the place. Then he would go back home to a house empty of everything but hungry children.

That's pretty much how it went day after day. And that's how it might have kept on going until, one morning, Jacob, the rich man, did something he had never done before: He woke up, just for a moment, during the reading of the Torah. Why did Jacob wake up just then? Who knows? But he did— and just long enough to hear one verse from the Book of Leviticus: "You shall bake twelve loaves of challah, and set them before Me in two rows, six in each row." That was it. Then he yawned and fell back to sleep.

When the service was over, Jacob rubbed his eyes and swallowed hard. The sound of the words was still so clear in his ears that he was sure it must have been God who had spoken to him. "But why to me of all people?" he wondered. "And why twelve loaves of bread? On the other hand, who am I to question God?" So Jacob, the rich man, hurried home across the square and baked twelve loaves of challah.

But now he had a problem: How to get the bread to God? He decided that the synagogue was the holiest place he knew. So he put the loaves of challah in a sack and carried them back to the synagogue.

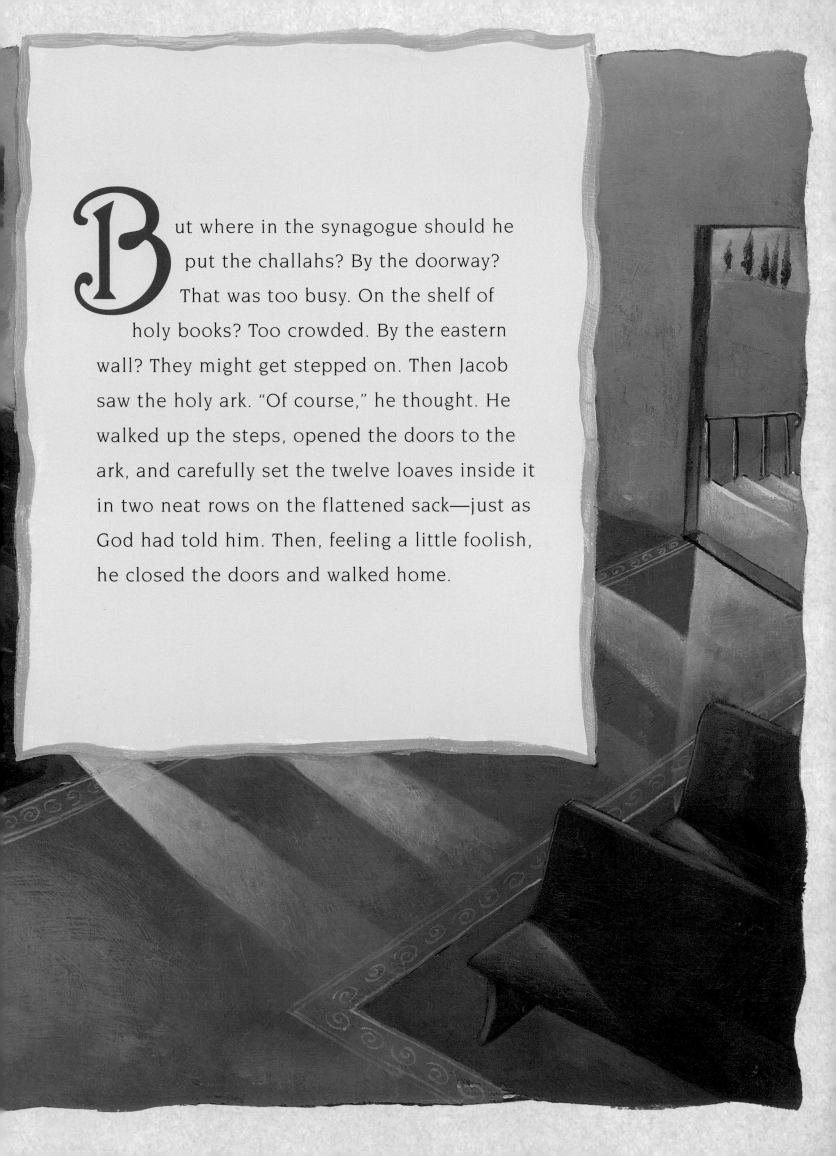

But where in the synagogue should he put the challahs? By the doorway? That was too busy. On the shelf of holy books? Too crowded. By the eastern wall? They might get stepped on. Then Jacob saw the holy ark. "Of course," he thought. He walked up the steps, opened the doors to the ark, and carefully set the twelve loaves inside it in two neat rows on the flattened sack—just as God had told him. Then, feeling a little foolish, he closed the doors and walked home.

No sooner had Jacob left than David, the poor man, came into the synagogue to clean up. He swept, he dusted, and he tidied. Then he stopped in front of the holy ark. His family had so little and he was so hungry. "O God," he prayed, "we are out of food. O Lord of infinite wisdom and compassion, I am afraid that if You do not see fit to help us soon, we shall starve."

Then he opened the doors of the ark. And there they were: twelve loaves of challah!

"O God," David said, "I didn't know You worked like that! Blessed are You, O Lord our God, who answers the prayers of those who call upon You in need!" Overjoyed, he gathered the twelve loaves into the sack and ran home to show his wife and children the bread from heaven.

No sooner had he left than Jacob, the rich man, came back into the empty synagogue, curious to see if God really ate challahs. He slowly approached the ark and opened its doors. The challahs were gone! "Oh, my God," he whispered. "God, You really ate the challahs! It's a miracle! I thought you were only kidding. Please forgive me: I wasn't sure it was really You, so I scrimped on the eggs. This is wonderful. Next week, I will be back here with twelve new loaves, and this time, I'll spare no expense!" He closed the doors of the ark and ran home to tell his family that God had accepted their gift.

So the next week, just as he had promised, Jacob, the rich man, brought to the synagogue twelve new loaves of challah— and this time with raisins! He placed them in two neat rows inside the ark. "Praised are You, O Lord our God," he said, "who accepts the gifts of those who offer them in love."

No sooner had Jacob left than David, the poor man, came in.

"O God," he prayed, "we have eaten all the challahs You gave us and some we have given away to those less fortunate. But now there is nothing left again. I know I should not ask, and I hope you won't think me greedy, but do You think, in Your infinite compassion …" (He slowly approached the ark as he spoke.) … "You could somehow see fit to bestow on Your servant another small gift? Perhaps just one more tiny miracle?"

He opened the doors of the ark and, sure enough, there were twelve loaves of challah—and this time with raisins, too! "Another miracle, and even better than the first!" cried David. "This is wonderful. Praised are You, O Lord our God, who answers the prayers of those who call upon You in truth!" He scooped up the loaves and ran home to share God's gift with his wife and children.

And so it went. Week after week, Jacob, the rich man, brought twelve loaves of challah to the ark as a gift for God. And week after week, David, the poor man, brought home twelve loaves of challah from the ark as a gift from God.

The weeks grew into months, and the months, years. Jacob's giving and David's receiving became a routine thing. The rich man would run into the empty synagogue with a sack of challahs and just throw them into the ark. And no sooner did he leave than the poor man would run in and scoop up the challahs and shout, "Thanks, God."

Then, one day, the rabbi happened to come back into the prayer hall late one afternoon and watch the whole amazing thing. Astonished, the rabbi called Jacob and David back and told them what he had seen. Jacob and David were astonished, too. "The holy ark is not some kind of heavenly bakery!" said the rabbi.

"I should have known: God doesn't eat challah," said Jacob, his voice now low and sad. "There wasn't any miracle after all."

"I should have known: God doesn't bake challah either," said David, his voice low and sad, too. "There wasn't any miracle after all."

"You are correct. God does not eat challah. And God does not bake challah," said the rabbi with a kindly smile. "God's miracles are not like that."

Then the rabbi took their hands in his. "Now that you know that God does not eat challah and God does not bake challah, you will have to do something even harder. Jacob, you will have to go on baking the bread anyway. David, you will have to go on eating the bread also. Now you understand that your hands are God's hands."

Jacob and David looked at their hands and then they looked into each other's faces. They understood.

Now Jacob and David often come to the synagogue together. They sit side by side. Jacob does not fall asleep during prayers, and David's belly does not growl from hunger. After prayers, they come out and stand together in the warm sunshine.

If you were there, you might see them—two men standing together, looking at one another. Two men who understand that their hands are the hands of God.